Ecuador

Climbing Volcanos

Stephen and Scharlie Platt

www.leveretpublishing.com

Ecuador Climbing Volcanos
First published - April 2017
Second Edition - September 2017
Published by
Leveret Publishing
56 Covent Garden, Cambridge, CB1 2HR, UK

ISBN 978-1-9124600-2-1

Ecuador
Climbing Volcanos

ECUADOR 1990

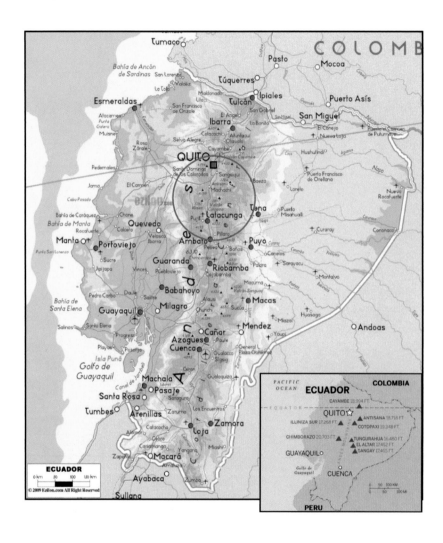

Caracas (950m)

After a fourteen-hour flight we were met by Hans, Cecilia, Ramon and Flor at Maiquetia airport and stay up till 3am chatting.

Sunday 25 November

We went rock climbing with Ramon, Flor and Hugo Arnal and I climbed Titanic at La Guairita with Marcos, the first ascensionist.

The Avila, the mountain range that separates Caracas from the coast, looks lush just now with large areas of heather pink oil grass. Cecilia, Hans' wife, is a landscape designer and Scharlie talked with her about how the planting in the city seems sensitive and beautiful.

Titanic, La Guairita (5.8, 5b)

Quito (2,850 m) and Loma Lumbisi (3,039 m)

Monday 26 November
Evening flight to Quito and we are met by an excited Fran and Sophie. Scharlie is feeling the altitude with headache and racing heart and Steve seems to have gastric flu. We spend a quiet day getting money and settling in.

Tuesday 27 November
We walk up the Loma Lumbisi, a grassy ridge on the east side of the city. There is clear blue sky all day and it is serene and green on the hill. We pass a family of pigs and a young man, washing clothes in companionable silence with his elderly mother. There are hardly any indigenous trees at this height except in

the hedges and below us, and in isolated eucalyptus groves. The hills are terraced for maize, potatoes, beans and flowers. Packs of well-fed friendly dogs come and say hello.

The views of Quito make the ascent worthwhile, but the last two hours of the walk are hard going; very hot with little shade and an uncertain path. We cross the Machángara River, a raging torrent of brown stench and catch the bus back from Guápulo, a

Loma Lumbisi, Quito

cobbled village with a famous church, La Virgen de Guadelupe, which we don't have time to see as the bus is just leaving. On the bus we are entertained by a local wag who mimes and mimics from the back of the bus. Omelettes for supper and early bed.

Wednesday 28 November

A lazy day and all four of us go into the old city. We arrive late at midday, just as all the museums close and eat watermelon in the park. On the way home Scharlie notices her bag has been slashed and her camera is gone. Pilar came round at five bearing a chocolate cake. She is vivacious and naturally friendly.

Thursday 29 November

We trek into the old city again to report the stolen camera. The police are helpful and quick in spite of the bureaucracy of quadruple typed copies. We go to Pilar and Pepe's for lunch. They lend us their driver and Jeep for the afternoon while Fran and Sophie have gone off to the beach by bus.

Calle García Moreno, Quito

Rumiñahui (4,721 m) Stone Eye / Rock Face

Atahualpa's half-brother, who led resistance against the Spanish in 1533.

Friday 30 November, Limpiapungo 3,300m.

We catch a bus and then a taxi towards Cotopaxi. Our driver Gonzales leaves us by Limpiopungo, a shallow lake noted for water birds and a black toad. We walk round the north-east side of the lake and stop for lunch. We feel lethargic and although it is only 2:30 Steve wants to stop and camp about a kilometre further on where we have a fine view of Cotopaxi.

We plan to climb Ruminahui tomorrow and Scharlie is for pushing on a bit higher, using more of the day and reducing the walk-in tomorrow. So we move on a kilometre or so and sit by a babbling stream that is flowing swiftly in a trench out through the soft turf. It proves to be our undoing. The grass is full of saxifrage and wild flowers and, between the clouds, the sun is hot. We have the rest of the day to kill and Steve is feeling lethargic. When he stands up, he can feel the effects of the altitude. Scharlie leaves her sack and goes up the trail to prospect and when she returns we decide to stop here.

The stream was fast flowing and sunk nearly a yard down in the grassy turf but only 8 inches wide at the rim. While Scharlie is inside the tent testing how comfortable the ground is, a flurry of wind picked up her anorak and tossed

Ruminahui and Lago Limiopungo

it together with our guidebook and deodorant into the stream. Steve dives to grab them and catches the anorak but the guidebook is whisked away underground. Tantalisingly, it reappears twice but too fast for us to catch. We spend an hour or two poking with sticks but all we recover is some small pieces of paper about Cotopaxi. Bed at 6 pm and sleep twelve hours straight through.

Saturday 31 November
Our valley wasn't lit by the sun till 7 so we are slow getting packed and don't set off till after 8. We both feel energetic compared to yesterday when even a small walk up the hillside was exhausting.

We hide the stove, pans and food under hairy grass and set off NW up the valley towards Ruminahui, following a way up through the vegetation. We climb up the south side of the valley, contouring along, but the trail gets narrower and disappears and we can see the path below us on the flat valley floor. We are out of breath with the altitude, but going fairly well. Feeling uncomfortable that we are off route we finally drop down to the path losing 100m altitude.

It takes took two hours to walk up the valley to a wide grassy plain under the mountain where a herd of wild horses led by a black stallion are feeding. There are two or three types of bushes growing up to 8 feet high and the turf underfoot is springy and full of alpine flowers – gentians, alchemilla, geraniums

are some of the plants we recognise. Having lost our guide we haven't a clue which way to climb the mountain.

Ruminahui (4,800m) is a rock mountain with three or four distinct summits running in a line about a mile long generally south-north with steep rotten cliffs. We remembered the guide had talked about wide grassy ledges and assumed these must be on the west side since we couldn't see any on the east. We can't decide whether to climb the ridge to our left and then contour round to the west side, climb a scree slope up to a col in the centre, or go up the ridge to our right. We decide to go straight up the middle to the col in the centre since this seemed the most obvious way to get to the ridge, and from there we assumed we could drop over to these ledges and reach each of the summits.

We leave our rucksacks under a distinctive bush glowing with scaly orange flowers just where it begins to get steep at the head of the valley. Even without the weight we have to stop to rest every 10 or 20 steps. The altitude makes our hearts batter and bang against our chests and breathing is as if we are sprinting. After about 500m Scharlie's head starts hurting and its odd that it hurts much more when we stop to rest. We climb up a vegetated ridge and work right towards the col wherever it seems convenient. As we reach the scree, which was soft volcanic earth, we keep to the left side under the cliffs where the going is firmer. Out of breath and feeling the altitude.

At the top there were no grassy ledges, just crumbling red towers and unstable rock and a long drop to the central valley. We rest and then traverse right towards the point where the right hand valley ridge joins the main mountain. A chasm separates us from the main summit, which is in cloud. We had hoped to find gentler slopes on the other side to enable us to skirt round to the summit but the cliffs drop sheer down to the valley about 2,000m below to scrub and then cultivated fields. We might have been able to scramble over the jagged ridge itself but the mist is coming in and the rock was anything but good – stones bound together by mud.

We waited half an hour for it to clear and got tantalising views of the slabby cliffs, We had taken only an hour and a half to get up and we sat on top about another hour before deciding to descend. What looked like scree below turned out to be sand, which you could descend as if it was snow. Scharlie's light shoes were not ideal for this as she couldn't use the heels to kick in and they filled with sand but it was quick and we made it down in half an hour. It was curious how close the summit seemed even after we had descended some distance. Only trees and bushes gave us a sense of scale and distance. We lay in the sun at the bottom but our heads were painful and the idea of a cup of tea was attractive.

A small herd of wild horses kept watch on us as we loaded our packs. The three mares, two foals and a beautiful grey stallion with a swishing black tail floated across the slope and disappeared in a few minutes with pounding hooves. It seemed a long way back to the campsite. The walk back down the valley was easy terrain but it seemed long.

Our heads began to really hurt on the descent. Steve was starting to shiver and feel sick. After an hour we reached our hidden cache by the stream and just had the energy to find the paracetamol and light the stove for tea.

Someone was already camped in our spot by the stream but after half an hour we felt recovered enough to walk over to a more open campsite and erect the tent.

A young American, Jason from Minnesota, was discreetly camped behind a hillock. He had been studying the lake for a week on an ecology project. We had not seen Condor but saw solitary smaller black vultures like Jamaican John Crow soaring high above the mountain. The American said they were Cara Cara.

Until recently, five to ten years ago, he said, a big black toad Sapo Ambato was common from Cayambe to Cotopaxi. They had been so plentiful it was hard not to step on one. It is now extinct in Limpiopungo. He doesn't know why. The lake has a lot of rubbish in it and, much to his surprise, the Ph changed from acid fifteen years ago (7.5) to basic now (6). He says there is a small farm in a beautiful green valley towards Sincholagna. There are waterfowl on the lake, but not as many as we expected.

The horses have torn up the turf in many places, perhaps to get at the roots, or maybe the stallions do it in the mating season. Scharlie is excited by the alpine flora.

Sunday 2 December

Our driver (we paid him 6,000 Sucre in advance to come back for us) turned up on the dot of 10am. Jason decided to come back with us. It took 2 1/2 hours. We washed clothes and rested.

Monday 3 December

After posting letters, buying books, etc., we go to Pilar and Pepe's for a lunch of calf's foot soup! Good for hangovers, they say. In the afternoon Pilar had Ricardo their driver, take us round the old city to the Church and Monastery of St. Francis, heavy with gold and pictures of Hell and Purgatory that Pilar used to be fascinated by as a child. The statue of the Virgin of Quito is chained and standing on a snake. I ask why. Pilar says that directly below the hill in the old town was a street of prostitutes and that the Virgin was chained so she wouldn't go down and join them.

Pilar left us at an exhibition of Ecuadorian crafts and from there we went to the Casa de Cultura to see if we could get tickets for the concert of guitar music by Riera and Suarez promoted by the Venezuelan Embassy. We were directed to speak with Licenciado Muñoz, director of public relations. He took us into his office and we talked at length about novels. His favourite is John Fowles "El Mago". He also gave us a list of Ecuadorian novels, which he said were basic.

The concert was good. The ambassador had a nice smile and his introduction was brief and good. Rafael Riera was very relaxed – playing guitars made by our friend Ramon Blanco. After, milling about in the foyer, the English are noticeably stiff, in contrast to the Latins hugging and parading around.

We return to the flat to find Hans has arrived and has the flat next door. He was hoping to meet with Randy and companions and film them hang-gliding from the mountains. They also want to climb all the volcanoes in Ecuador.

Ruccu Pichincha (4,698 m) *'Old Man'*

Tuesday 4 December

We decided to climb Pichincha with Hans. We had been thoroughly warned against it because of a bandit who had held up party of eight at gunpoint and left them with only their T-shirts! But Hans was determined and we're very glad we went as it was beautiful. We caught a taxi up through the barrio of Las Chorreras and we set off walking from the statue of the Virgin and then took winding paths through what we called 'bush' in Jamaica. Misty tangled vines and spicy smells, flowers and every now and then a hut on a hillside and carefully terraced fields growing maize or broad beans. Then on to the open mountain side above the antenna on Crux Loma.

The classical route detours where the path comes to a mini *quebrada* just too wide to jump. Then five miles of rolling ridge walk like the Lakes or the Pennines. Hans walks very slowly and carefully and Scharlie found if she copied this and matched her steps to a rhythm of breathing with her hands clasped behind her back she could keep going without feeling sick or out of breath. If she missed the rhythm everything went ragged and the strength left her legs.

It made one feel it would be worth going to classes to get good at breathing control. At last we scrambled up the summit rocks, skirting the steepest part until we reached a scree slope and the top at 2pm.

We sit on the sandy earth surrounded by alpine flowers. The going was hard, but we feel better than on Ruminahui. We relax on top then leap up and start back as soon as thunder starts. We run for cover as an electric storm breaks. Steve's hair crackles and smokes. We race down the scree slope as quickly as possible and get down about 5 pm; tired but exhilarated. Six hours climb and three hours down and no sign of the bandit. Maybe he's got the day off for the fiesta.

At home we find the girls back from beach. After a hurried meal, we went to the Jacchigua ballet of folkloric Indian dancing at the Teatro Nacional. Hans didn't come as he was feeling sick. Wednesday was a rest day, shopping, and a fish lunch at Las Palimiros. Festival party in the Park – salsa dance beat exciting and the town of firework competition inventive and captivating bamboo structures with animation each one taking up to 15 minutes to unfold.

Baños

Baños (1,815 m)

Thursday 6 December.

Hans was sick in the night, probably from eating mussels, but ready to go to Baños in the morning. We are on the Pan-American Highway in the dusty outskirts of the city. Dogs playing and searching for food; cows eating the lead polluted verge grass; a llama rushing suddenly from a back garden; bright light; potholes and cobbles. Half-finished concrete-block houses with steel rod whiskers waggling on top. A beauty salon in a shack. Maize crop in neat ridges everywhere. Pastoral views out of town, green rolling grass, tall rows and clumps of eucalyptus. Cactus by the road but receding to hills as cool as the Pennines.

Steeply down to Baños to the Gertrudis hotel. Baños is a beautiful, quiet, gentle town surrounded by green mountains. Hans had remembered this hotel from when he'd stayed there with Cecilia. It was built in 1948 by a man

named Axel, a German Jew who had fled Nazi Germany. His wife's name was Gertrudis. It's timber, painted green and cream on the outside.

It's owned by Argentinians but in the charge of a decorous old man from Quito while they're on holiday. Long face the colour of a raspberry with a small purse of a mouth, dark amused eyes, slicked black hair, brown suit and with a gentle, shuffling competent manner. Yes, we can have rooms downstairs in the old part of the hotel. The dim cool interior delighted Scharlie with memories of Jamaica – sweet jasmine, begonias and Busy Lizzie's in pots crowded on the stone front steps. Inside wide polished boards, silky, gleaming. The floorboards are a good foot wide and glowed with years of polishing. The ceiling was also of wood and the window looked out onto the back garden and the mountain. Lying on the bed with the white light bright through the shutters, and glimpses of limestone cliffs startlingly green with forest vegetation. An avocado tree directly outside the window, cows in the pasture and a dog barking in the distance. Very quiet; a sensation of timelessness.

In the street outside the hotel Baños was hot, but with no noise of travel or smell of gasoline, only sounds of farming. We mooch around the wide streets using up time, making a phone call to Cecilia in a newly built concrete telephone temple with a step down just inside the door which Hans fell over twice. The telephonist sits behind a counter so high that it reached most Ecuadorians at eye level standing on tiptoe. The line so bad that all Hans manages is "Its me … yes … Randy who? No … well …okay, bye." We were too late for the hot springs, which shut at 4:30. They open at 5am so we vowed to get there early in the morning before catching the *camioneta* at the Patti at 9 to take us part of the way up the mountain. We dined in the hotel waited on by a waitress with a long pale face and a strict expression. She seems to run the place and changes into a black maid's outfit to serve dinner. Throughout the meal she stands stiffly in her starch uniform. She seemed to do all the work but at a curious, unhurried pace as if she were in a dream.

Tungarahua (5,023 m) *'Throat of Fire'*

Friday 7 December
Tungarahua is an active volcano towering over Baños. It's an awful mountain to climb in summer, being composed of 2,000m of loose ash.

We crowded into the Patti with a couple of voluble Americans and a tall

silent German couple. Later we found they were called Norbert and Sabina and they spoke French, English and Spanish. They had taken three months off from studying near Frankfurt. We got a lorry at 9am to take us to Pondoa from where we began the walk to the refuge. We paid $2 to the *guardia parque* to enter the Tungarahua park and $1 each to use the refuge.

The track climbed through grassy meadows and then, furrowed by the passage of many feet, it narrowed to a tunnel roofed with bamboo and liana. There is a worn channel three feet deep in places where people and horses have worn a deep rut. It was cool and there were lots of flowers and plants.

It took us about two and a half hours to reach the refuge (3,800m) which was small and well situated on a level bit of the ridge a few hundred feet below where the vegetation ended. We found a patch of grass below the hut, and having bagged two places in the sleeping room upstairs, stretched out in the afternoon sunshine.

About five, we could hear loud pop music, and a party of eight or nine young

Steep rutted path to refuge

Ecuadorians arrived carrying a ghetto blaster. There was the usual tension in any refuge when a large party arrives after everyone has settled in and the refuge seems full. In fact, they turned the radio down low when asked and were nice lads.

We cooked soup, then rice with one of Han's dried meals. We got to bed

Refuge Tungarahua

about nine o'clock, and slept till 11, but were woken by someone going to the loo. Everyone was a bit worried about their belongings. Hans said, careful with the camera and later, in the night, we heard a big careful movement and someone say "*mochilas*", which means rucksack and we came wide awake, listening to see if they were ransacking our gear. In the event, we had no need to worry.

Saturday 8 December

We got up at 2 a.m. and left the hut about 3.30, after making breakfast of bread and cheese and pints of rose hip tea that Hans recommended. The ash was frozen, but with every few steps the ground would collapse like soft icing and you would slip down.

Scharlie had only a slight headache and sickness and felt reasonably energetic. She tried her plastic boots but gave up after two steps and decided to carry them. Her red Ecco trainers had taken a new lease of life with a pair of white inner soles. The first hour was a gasping nightmare. We climbed loose lava unsound, with no purchase for the feet. We sunk and floundered and slid backwards. It was steep and the weight of Scharlie's rucksack pulled her off. After a while Steve relieved her of the water which helped. Hans kept steadily on with his ski sticks. Scharlie followed his zigzag route with her head torch. Steve saved his. Gradually we regained frozen ground and outcrops of rock that gave firmer footing.

After about two hours we reach the snow line, which should look sunnier in the day. The snow was thin and loose rock poked through. A large boulder thundered down, dislodged by two Americans who had overtaken us. The young Ecuadorians passed us in a line in the dark, sure-footed, flashing their torches occasionally. At 5:30am we hear someone call out high above us the "morning is coming!" And so we went on, zigzag torch beam, on Hans' heels, unnecessary as the sky lightened. Breathing deeply some rhythm possible on the frozen ground and snow. Now deeper, slipping sinking losing balance, breathing ragged. Continuous sick headache; numbing determination.

Finally we reach the rim of the crater in the blue morning, long after the sun had risen, after being overtaken by everyone who had set off after us. Only one person turned back, an older American called Scott. We could hear him cursing and swearing a few hundred feet below us, banging the earth with his ice axe before turning back. Scharlie thought he must have dropped something, but Steve said he was suffering from altitude, because he'd heard him retching all the way up.

At the crater, we put on our crampons, but because we had left the ice axes in Baños, Scharlie didn't want to climb the ridge – her legs felt wobbly and

Ridge on Tungarahua

she felt insecure. We crossed the crater and climbed the central slope where steps had been cut and the snow was softer. The smell of sulphur encouraged us. Hans took the more spectacular route up the steep exposed ridge People were coming down. The young Ecuadorians covered in smiles descending the icy slope in their rubber boots with wooden sticks. Slowly we made it to the top without a problem and reached the summit at 9.30 am.

A little chocolate was all that interested us although we had brought bread

and ham. The altitude takes away appetite. We were lucky that the clouds were holding off and all the snowy mountain tops were clear around us. Below the snow sloped off the crater peaks like thick dripping cream.

The clouds were only just beginning to develop and we could see Chimborazo, Cotopaxi and Antisina in the north and El Altar to the south. Scharlie, without her axe, found the steep initial slope down from the summit, difficult.

It was a long walk down the ash fields, and Scharlie and Hans had problems

Tungarahua summit

with their boots – Hans getting a bad blister and Scharlie a bruised big toe. She said her shirt and thermal underclothes were plenty warm on the way up and she was able to strip off layers on the way down. She might have preferred a front zip but then she wouldn't have the large front pocket.

We stopped for half an hour at six, dizzy with weariness and got a little rest and drink then on down to the lorry that was coming at 2.30pm and wouldn't wait. When we reached the meadows Steve went ahead to catch the carrier, which he just managed. We could then sit and be carried to the rest of the way, burning muscles unwinding. On the drive down, one of the American rucksacks fell off the lorry, which ran over it, breaking the guy's camera and ripping his sac.

Back to Baños in time for the hot soothing spa water; beers at the cafe Allemagne and dinner at the Petit Français. The restaurant was celebrating its second birthday and there was a folk band. We ordered artichoke, followed by fondue. After beers we could hardly keep our eyes open and fell asleep three or four times sitting at the table, talking. We made it back to the hotel in a dream.

Baños Again (1,815 m)

Sunday 9 December

The following day, we spent at the baths, soaking until our fingers were all wrinkled. Again, we ate in the French restaurant, this time with two young Germans – Sabina, a biomedic and Norbert, an engineer from lower Saxony.

Gertrudis has become a home for home, restful, quiet and familiar. Anything could grow here in this climate avocado and peaches, date palms and hollyhocks. On the whole, the gardens in Ecuador do not exploit the variety of native plants that do well here. Where the forest has been left, the flowers and trees flourish but around here the hills are cleared for agriculture and only eucalyptus and pine planted in quantity. In the city there are few acacia and I have spotted some street trees that look like ash. Another thing we find remarkable is the number of dogs running about unleashed but apparently well fed and friendly with each other and strangers. If animals are unafraid it says a lot about the people.

The hot springs were lovely in the early morning mist. We took a taxi there

Thermal baths at Baños

and back. They are so cheap and efficient. Generally the taxis don't run on the clock but you soon get a feel for how much a journey should cost and you can refuse the taxi or bargain.. They have made concrete pools to hold the water as it gushes from the mountain cliffs which rise vertically from the baths. The water smells of sulphur and leaves a yellow brownish deposit so the concrete looks like stone. A cold mountain stream tumbles nearby and its water is used to control the temperature of the hot water so some pools are hotter than others. Most of the other clients are Ecuadorian, many rheumatic or old or fat. Sulphur acts as a disinfectant!

One hour's drive up a bruising road to Pondoa where there was a hut at the entrance to the Tungarahua park. We paid three dollars to the Guardian to enter the park and use the refuge. The road has been completed in the last two years. The Government paid a lump sum to the villagers to pave it by hand with stone cobbles, a beautiful job. When the rainy season comes torrents cross the road and they had been washed away. The road was closed entirely a few months ago. November to January is the season of flowers. The sun was hot and orchids shone from the dry spiky grass. Above Pondoa we started on the walk to the refuge – fortunately at that time in the morning

in the cool shadow of the mountain. Tunnels cut as deep as the height of the white horse that pushed on in front of us to carry the replacement gas cylinder to the hut. Moss and ferns growing from the moist brown banks. Bamboo bending over our heads. Plush gleaming tropical leaves and flowers – orange, red, yellow, pink and blue of lupin's.

Scharlie felt frustrated at her lack of botanical knowledge and no camera. She would have liked to give a lecture when we returned.

After a while the excitement of seeing so many beautiful plants restored her humour and gave her energy for the steep climb. We met

Steep climb to Tungaragua hut

28

Scharlie was fascinated by the plant life and frustrated by her lack of botanical knowledge

people coming down. The refuge was nearer than we thought; it has only taken two and a half hours.

We rest and cook soup and rice, listening to the chat of the Americans lying in the sun, watching the darkness deepen. Cotopaxi towers above the line of grey mountains, red in the sunset. Lights in the valley pricking out the valley floor as the darkness deepens. Where did all the houses come from? Sleep about nine.

A party of teenage Ecuadorian lads arrived with a ghetto blaster. They were full of good humour and happy to sleep downstairs since all the foreigners had bagged the sleeping area upstairs. Their gear was so home-made compared to ours. Blankets and sacks, torches, tennis shoes and wellies. They pass round *claudias* (plums) which helps to dispel the tension caused by their noisy arrival.

They cooked chicken stew and played cards quietly by candlelight while we went to bed. An intelligent looking black dog with brown patches who obviously considers the refuge to be his personal hunting territory has gone outside in the moonlight. He likes sitting on a promontory taking in the scenery. After a trip to the loo at 11.30, we slept well.

Carihuairazo (5,018 m) *'Man Wind Snow'*

Carihuairazo was first climbed by Edward Whymper and the brothers Louis and Jean-Antoine Carrel during their 1880 Ecuador expedition.

Monday 10 December

Hans had arranged to go to Carihuairazo with his friends Norbert and Sabina and Carlos from the Patti, would take us in a truck, leaving at 6am. Scharlie and Sabina travelled in the cab with Carlos, while Steve and Hans suffered the cold in the open back of the truck. It was freezing with long icicles hanging by the road, although the sun was bright.

The road from Ambato climbed to 9,000m. We turned off the main Guaranda road at Rio Blanco and drove to the first locked gate, where Carlos walked over to talk to the Indians who tended a herd of 130 vicuñas imported from Bolivia by the Ministry of Agriculture in an attempt to reintroduce the species to Chimborazo.

Paying 1500 cash, we were allowed through, and the man rode with us to

5 000 m
CARIHUAIRAZO

the second gate. Here we saw a group of vicuñas in the distance. Soft, beige animals running at the noise of the lorry. We drove three to four miles further until the road got too bad, and then we set off walking.

10.15 p.m. I wanted to strike off up a valley leading straight from the small lake below the road towards the mountains, but Hans wanted to follow the road to the path on his map. We were sure Carlos had said to head straight up to the left of the ridge, but Hans was unconvinced.

Below Chimborazo, there was another lake and a shepherd tending a large flock of sheep. They work the sheep without dogs, which seem to be kept only as guards. Keeping to the high ground, we contoured around the left side of the valley with the lake where the guidebook had recommended that we camp.

We reached the snow and put on crampons. Scharlie's toe was still very sore and she felt head achy and so decided not to climb. Hans put Sabina and Norbert in the middle of the rope and we set off about 1.15 pm. There was a patch of ice soon after we had started, which we had to traverse. They slipped and Hans cut steps. From there to the summit ridge was straightforward and we zigzagged up. We had to stop for a breather every zig, but we made good progress. There was some stone fall from the summit area, and as we reached

Climbing Carihuairazo

the skyline, the snow threatened to avalanche, producing tell-tale sheer lines. We only saw one crevasse, to our right about 200m below the ridge. We traversed along the ridge left to the rocky summit and there were two steps of four or five metres where we had to climb. Steve climbed first, not bothering to take off his crampons, fixed a belay and brought up the others.

The summit was tiny and Scharlie said later that she had seen us sticking out at angles like ninepins. It must have been when we were trying to take photos. We got down very quickly in 45 minutes, starting slowly, but Hans said they were fine skiing down, so Steve set a spanking pace. Norbert complained later that he had been dragged.

We met Scharlie half way back along the walk to the lorry. Steve had been following her footsteps and was confused when they seemed to diverge from

Summit Carihaurazo

our way up. She had gone right to prospect the alternative route, which we decided to take. We got back to the road near the lake under Chimborazo about 5 pm and had to walk a mile or so back to where Carlos was waiting. I had to use dark glasses as goggles to keep the dust out of my eyes. The light on Carihuairazo and Chimborazo was spectacular. We wrapped up as warm as we could. It was very cold and there were icicles on the road to Ambato.

Descent from Carihaurazo

Norbert thought the hotel Mirafiores was too expensive at 7000s. So Steve suggested we go back to the Gertrudis in Baños.

We got back at 9pm and changed quickly and went to the Restaurant Alemania. We had Hungarian soup and a 'plato fitness' which was a monster salad. We were all falling asleep at the table. Got to bed about 10.30.

Hacienda La Cienaga, Latacunga (3,003 m)

Avenue to Hacienda La Cienaga, built by Don Matheo de la Escalera y Velasco in 1695

Tuesday 11 December 1990

Went to the bank and telephoned Fran. Then we had an hour in the baths at the Piscina de la Virgin before packing and setting off. Hans had befriended a shoe shine boy called Guenersindo in the Patti and I let him clean my boots, telling him if he made a good job of them he could do my shoes.

He said he had no money for school. His father, he said, had been a drunkard and was killed walking on the road. He lived with his mother in a nearby village and worked at the Patti for 3,000 Sucres a week. Before, he said, a thousand Sucres had been a lot of money, but not now. He admired my watch – as have a number of other Ecuadorians.

We caught a bus very efficiently and were dropped off on the Pan American Highway at the gates of the Hacienda la Cienaga. A sign said 1 kilometre, but it seemed longer. The road was very dusty, but the fields were lush, and as we

Our 'four-poster bed' at Hacienda La Cienaga

arrived at the main avenue of eucalyptus up to the house, we could see the marshland that had given the house its name.

We were asked if we wanted a 'matrimonial' and were shown a four room suite by the porter. It was on the top floor, reached by a private spiral staircase. In the bedroom there was a mini four-poster bed and Victorian style prints of reclining nudes.

The next room was a drawing room with a writing desk, chandelier and balcony overlooking the main avenue to the main entrance. The cost was only 4,000 s more than that of a double. It must have been the patron's quarters and had seen better days. The bed-clothes were much too small for the bed and Scharlie and I fought each other for a scrap of blanket all night. Dozens of tables had been laid for dinner, but the other guests were huddled round the fire in the far room. The set meal was fair.

The party on the table next to ours were two middle-aged Germans and two younger Ecuadorians – parents and children maybe. They'd had an accident with the transmission of their rented Jeep and the old man had a face like thunder. He kept getting up from the table and walking out. Their dream trip wasn't going to plan. Hans was in good form, talking about Venezuela and Cecilia.

Cotopaxi (5,897 m) 'Neck of the Moon'

Cotopaxi is one of Ecuador's most active volcanoes

Tuesday 11 December 1990

After breakfast we dossed around, washing some clothes, etc. until lunchtime. We had booked the car for 2, but Hans had asked the receptionist to see if she could change it to 1. She had, but didn't tell us, and the carretera arrived half way through lunch. Hans and I settled ourselves in the back and we began the familiar drive into Cotopaxi. The car had a slipping clutch and made it with difficulty to the car park below the refuge.

We picked up a young chap in Limpiopungo who told us that Judy Leden had just flown from the top of Cotopaxi in a hang-glider, and that we had missed seeing her by an hour or so. They had spent three to four days acclimatising in the refuge. Ten climbers from Baños had carried the glider up to the summit and there had been three camera crews. Our young man hadn't made it, being unused, he said, to carrying heavy loads.

We cooked and got to bed soon after 6pm. By light, Steve's worst fears were realised when the group downstairs started singing in celebration of their

The Jose F. Rivas refuge (4800m) is the most popular refuge in Ecuador

success. It was after eleven and we just got off to sleep when Hans went down and asked them if they were climbing that morning and if not they should let those that were, sleep.

We got up soon after 1.30am and left the hut about 3.30.am The first part was easy, up a long stretch of volcanic ash before the snow and up to where the mountain steepens. We stopped and put on our crampons and roped up, Hans in the lead, then Scharlie and Steve at the back. From here it was like walking up an unrelenting steep ice staircase for hour after hour. You climb slowly and have to take care of your foot placement so as not to slip. In the dark your mind wanders and you concentrate on your breathing and putting one foot in front of another. The person at the back is the anchor. If someone slipped and fell you would need to thrust in your ice axe and take a belay to arrest the fall. Hans went very slowly, which suited Scharlie.

We crossed two crevasses, both with snow bridges and neither more than a stride's width. We passed Yanisacha, the black rock, as dawn broke.

The Ecuadorian team passed us just before their camp in a hollow immediately before the last steep section. They had two dome tents there as an advanced base camp. About here we began to feel the altitude as we traversed leftwards to the horizon on 50 degrees of snow.

Climbing Cotopaxi

The sun began to fill the horizon and our spirits lifted with the light. We rested out of the wind on a flat section behind a huge ice tower. There was a short ice wall where you needed to use your ice axe and then an exposed ridge, where the wind put you off balance. There were two more false summits which were very trying before we reached the top (5800m) at 11.30am after eight hours climbing, .

Looking down from the summit into the mouth of the crater

Summit of Cotopaxi (5897m)

Looking back at the snow packed trail, we could see the route of our climb. The peak of Cotopaxi rises above the main crater and peering over the edge, we had a view down right into the crater. Steve felt very tired and just wanted to sit. Scharlie had a mild attack of hysterics – laughing and hugging us both. I sat on my rucksack, breaking my snow goggles. We were very slow on the descent. Scharlie's legs felt wobbly. I went in front and Hans took the rear. Hans and I headed straight down while Scharlie zig-zaged As the snow got softer in the sun, the snow balled up under her crampons, making it seem she was walking in Japanese platform sandals. She fell once or twice but stopped herself in the soft snow. Hans was very quick and would have held her on the rope.

We reached the hut sometime after 2pm, having watched our driver arrive at the parking place. Steve repacked the rucksacks. It was very tiring just climbing the stairs to get the gear we'd left in the locker upstairs. Our driver wanted extra for the hour's delay. We offered 1,000, he wanted 5,000. We settled on 2,000. Again Hans and Steve sat muffled up in the back. As we passed Limpiopungo, we could see the hang-glider expedition sorting out their gear outside the military refuge. The Baños lads passed us on the road to Lasso. We caught a bus and left the climbers from Baños still waiting on the other side of the road.

At first Scharlie and Steve had to sit on the engine and nodded off to sleep.

Looking down from the summit into the mouth of the crater

44

Then two seats came free came free near Hans. Steve sat next to an Indian from near Cuenca who said he sold pouches and bags. He wanted to know our address so he could come round and show us. He looked scruffy and anyway it was the girls' flat. I told him it was impossible for him to come round that night, our daughter was cooking a meal and all we wanted was a bath and a beer. Finally, Scharlie said she wanted to go to Otavalo to buy her stuff, and so it wasn't convenient

Friday 14 December, p.m.
We had lunch with Hans at a restaurant called Pyms, and that evening went downtown to the Hotel Colon. On Avenida 10 de Agosto, near Avenida Naciones Unidas, there was a roadblock. Soldiers in helmets with automatic weapons were stopping the traffic and men in leather jackets were asking people to show their papers. We had agreed not to tell the taxi driver we were going to the Hotel Colon so he wouldn't charge us extra, but Sophie let it slip and we all laughed and walked straight in the front door since that was where he dropped us.

Hotel Colon Hilton, Avenida Patria, Quito

Chimborazo (6,268 m) 'Ice throne of God'

Chimborazo 6268m, highest mountain in Ecuador

Thought until the beginning of the 19th century to be the highest mountain on Earth, which led to many attempts on its summit during the 17th and 18th centuries. First climbed by Edward Whymper and his Italian guides Louis Carrel and Jean-Antoine Carrel in 1880.

Saturday 15 December

Fran, Sophie and Scharlie went to Otavalo and Hans and Steve went to get a bus to Ambato. Steve was feeling good and he'd got used to the altitude and felt happy about the gear. There were two loud-mouthed youths on the bus who had been out drinking the night before. They swore a bit and had the window open. I got something in my eye and felt useless when we got off the bus in Ambato, leaving Hans to fix up a lift to the refuge with the only truck around — a Toyota Camioneta. The driver was finishing his breakfast in the roadside café and we went and found him. On the road towards Guaranda,

Line of ascent

he had the stereo on and sang along to the exciting love songs. Hans had him stop to film llamas.

As we got nearer to the turn-off, he began to complain. Hans stayed cool and, when he recognised the turning, insisted that the driver follow his directions. The dirt road was excellent, wide, flat and an easy gradient. The man kept bleating about how he hadn't bargained on going so high, but we ignored him. At the restaurant below the refuge where we parked he got out a Polaroid camera and had his photo taken in front of Chimborazo. Having organised our packs and applied glacier cream to our lips, we set off at Hans' snail's pace to walk the half a mile to the hut. Halfway there, we were overtaken by a group we'd passed earlier in an army bus. They were a climbing club and had come for the weekend. Despite living on the coast, they were all fitter and more acclimatised than either Hans or Steve.

The refuge was clean and well kept. Hans had another slight contra-temp with the guardian about the cost I paid and got him to give us a receipt. Hans asked if there was a carbon copy left in his book. It seemed good value to me. The bunk-room was quiet. We were sharing with a party of three French. The girl was suffering badly from the altitude and decided not to climb – so only one of the men went with the two guides they had contracted from Riobamba.

The Whymper refuge at 5,000 m is Ecuador's highest-altitude mountain refuge

Steve made Hans lots of soup and got to bed early, using Sophie's ear-plugs for the first time and slept really well – waking naturally about 11 pm. We geared up and breakfasted and everything looked good for a successful ascent. Outside it was cold and there was a strong northerly wind. Steve was wearing Scharlie's top and two vests and despite the wind, felt warm enough although his feet were cold. We were the second or third party away and although we went very slowly, as usual, we seemed to be making steady progress. On the ridge the wind became even stronger, threatening to blow us over at times. We were still on scree and rock and there seemed very little snow in the ice runnels above us.

Others had passed us and we could see the lights of their head torches. Hans suggested we should rope up and we dropped over the other side of the ridge to get out of the gale. Steve found it incredibly irksome to break out of the rhythm of slogging upwards. The whole business of tying on and coiling the rope in the way Hans wanted, he found cumbersome and just putting the crampons on was a trial, seeming to take forever. However, we managed it all and set off again with Hans leading the way.

The ground was still very easy, although the wind just as fierce, and we still had some way to go before we reached the rock band where the real climbing started. We had been going fifteen or twenty minutes when Hans suddenly

Climbing Chimboazo

said he didn't want to go any further. Steve couldn't quite believe what he was saying at first. He felt pretty good and much better than he had on Cotopaxi, and was looking forward to actually having to climb. It also seemed such a waste, all the preparation, building up slowly one peak at a time, organising the equipment, getting a good night's sleep. Yet he just said 'Okay'. He had such a warm feeling for Hans, because he'd come out to spend time with us and he looked so worn out all of a sudden, as though he'd been carrying the burden of it all. Perhaps Steve should have tried to talk him into carrying on if he'd taken the lead and encouraged him. But he remembered how adamant Hans had always been when they used to climb together in Venezuela. Hans suggested Steve could go on and join one of the other parties, but he didn't fancy that since none of the Ecuadorians had looked that competent on ice. In fact, we learnt later that there was an Englishman and a Swiss in the lead party who made it to the top, although we didn't see them come back the following morning. As we stood dithering in the cold, parties ahead of us started to retreat, having been unable to climb the rock band because of the ice. Steve undid the rope from around his waist and bundled it into his sac.

We lost the track on the way down and would have missed the refuge had not Hans insisted we climb up and find the path. We went straight back to bed and slept another four hours until 7.30 or 8.

At the car park, we met up with the two guides, father and son and their French client called Etienne and persuaded a couple in a truck to give us a lift to Riobamba, via San Carlos. Hans said it was a beautiful place to camp, but either because of Steve's mood or the cloudy weather, he though it looked grey and uninteresting but then so had Limpiopungo from the road.

We caught the bus to Quito after only a short wait and got a seat near the front. Somewhere near Latacunga an old couple got on and sat on the engine cowling in front of us. Getting on these buses between towns was always a scramble with the driver's mate making a production of hurrying people. Maybe the woman tripped on a sack of produce that was sitting in the way, or maybe she just stumbled on the steps, but as she tried to stop herself falling, she dropped the baby she had wrapped in a shawl at her breast. It fell forward in an arc and although Steve was too far away, he moved forward instinctively to catch its naked body before its head hit the steel floor. In flight, he realised it was a doll. The woman took it from him and wrapped the blanket round it. To pay the fares,
she had to reach under her top for
a money pouch that she'd fashioned from a strip of cotton. She handed the baby to her husband, who seemed quite accustomed to nursing the doll. At first glance, he seemed dapper – dressed in a suit, tie and trilby hat. Only on closer inspection did we realise that his flies were undone and that the seams of the jacket were unravelling.

The couple got off and their seat on the engine was taken by another old man in a blazer and pork pie felt hat. Again, he seemed dapper and had a jaunty air about him. He asked for a ticket to Lasso and then later, having lit

Typical highly decorated bus

a cigarette, talking to himself to bolster his confidence, asked the driver to drop him off between stops on the *paramo* north of the town. The driver refused, saying that this was an express bus. Maybe they were already behind schedule. The old man ranted and raved – at first confident and bold, but then cowed and pathetic. At Lasso, he refused to get off and it looked as though he would get taken on as far as Machache. However, at the entrance to the park, someone flagged down the bus and the old man gleefully disembarked practically falling down the steps as the bus pulled away.

Quito (2,850 m)

Monday 17 December

The following morning, I got up at 6am to help Hans down with his luggage and to say goodbye. Fran had cooked supper and Hans and I had both been tired and subdued. The caretaker came down with us to unlock the door and asked Hans for his other key. Hans told him he had only been given one key. The old man said he must have lost it. Hans got irritated and lectured him on how disorganised they were about the keys and how they should have spares for all the flats.

They stood arguing the toss in front of the locked gate, until I wondered whether Hans would miss his plane. Finally, Hans got rattled and told him to unlock the gate and let him out. We hailed a cab and I gave him a hug and said goodbye.

Later we visited HCJB, The Voice of the Andes, the first radio station with daily programming in Ecuador and the first Christian missionary radio station in the world. Founded in 1931 by Stuart Clark, a close relative of Scharlie's. It broadcasted in English, Spanish and indigenous languages and they had just installed their first HC-100 (100,000-watt) transmitter when we were there.

HCJB 'The Voice of the Andes' Christain radio station

Papallacta (3,300 m)

Wednesday 18-19 December

We went with Fran and Sophie and stayed the night. We had our sleeping bags, but Fran and Sophie were cold in the night. So they left the hut and climbed into the warm spa to get warm. We joined them just as it was getting light. It was very atmospheric in the pale light of dawn and heavy mist enshrouded the hot pools. We slid into the milky water and luxuriated in the warmth. Quietly and rather magically an Indian family left one of the huts far below us and began to wind their way up a narrow dirt path towards the pools. The husband came first, then the wife, then the eight children in a line, strictly ordered by age and height. This must be their early morning ablution, usually conducted in complete privacy at this early hour. They noticed us with a start when they were almost upon us, since only the tops of our heads were visible above the water and we were shrouded in mist. They moved on to a pool above us and began to play very quietly and convivially.

Hot springs near Otavalo on the road from Quito down to the jungle, below Antisana (5,704 m). In 1990 it was it was quite primitive and unspoilt,

Saturday 21 December
Plane delayed. We fly back to the UK.

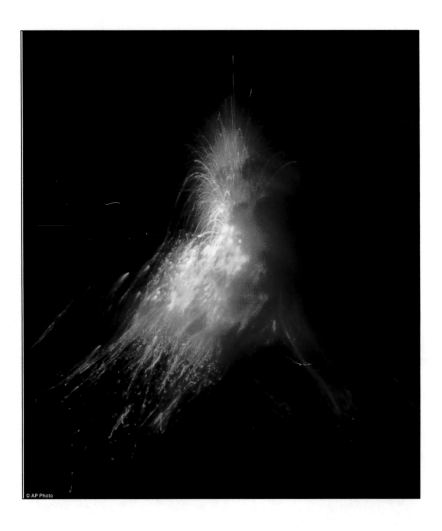

© AP Photo

Made in the USA
Columbia, SC
14 November 2019

83241150R00031